THE CONFESSING CHURCH
a play in two acts

by
Rachel Lulich

WordCrafts Theatrical

WordCrafts Theatrical Press

The Confessing Church
Copyright © 2021, Rachel Lulich
All Rights Reserved

CAUTION: Professionals and amateurs are hereby warned that performance of *The Confessing Church* is subject to payment of a royalty. It is fully protected under the copyright laws of the United States of America, and of all countries covered by the International Copyright Union. All rights, including professional, amateur, motion picture, public reading, broadcast, and any other reproduction by means known or yet to be discovered are strictly reserved.

All rights are controlled exclusively by WordCrafts Theatrical Press, 912 East Lincoln Street, Tullahoma, Tennessee 37388. No performance of this play may be given without obtaining in advance the written permission of WordCrafts Theatrical Press, https://www.wordcrafts.net/performance-rights-request, and paying the requisite fee.

SPECIAL NOTE

Anyone receiving permission to produce *The Confessing Church* is required to give credit to the Author as the sole and exclusive Author of the Play on the title page of all programs distributed in connection with performances of the Play and in all instances in which the title of the Play appears for purposes of advertising, publicizing or otherwise exploiting the Play. The name of the Author must appear on a separate line, in which no other name appears, immediately beneath the title and in size of type equal to 50% of the size of the largest, most prominent letter used for the title of the Play. No person, firm or entity may receive credit larger or more prominent than that accorded the Author.

All rights reserved. No part of this book may be reproduced, stored in a retrieval system, or transmitted in any form or by any means—electronic, mechanical, photocopy, recording, or otherwise—without the prior written permission of the publisher. The only exception is brief quotations for review purposes.

Published by WordCrafts Theatrical Press
912 E. Lincoln St. Tullahoma, Tennessee 37388
www.wordcrafts.net

Playwright's Notes

Crowd scenes (classroom, church, etc.) should be supplemented by additional actors.

All names should be pronounced as they are in German, with the exception of Luther, due to the extensive familiarity of the English pronunciation of his name.

Two sources were used for biblical quotes: The King James translation, and the Luther translation. Where the two differed, the playwright favored her own English translation of the Luther Bible. This is the reason 1 Peter 3:15 is herein given as 1 Peter 3:15-16.

The words "chapter" and "verse" should only be used where spelled out in dialog; otherwise, only the numbers should be pronounced. For example, 2 Timothy 1:7 is read "Second Timothy one seven." 1 Peter 3:13-15 is "First Peter three, thirteen through fifteen." "Two Timothy" instead of "second" is appropriate if the play is being produced in a place where that reading is common.

The offensive language used by the Nazi-leaning characters is closely modeled on the rhetoric of the time. Likewise, the language used in the church scenes is modeled on actual sermons by Confessing Church pastors. The contradiction of positively comparing Hitler to the Apostle Paul, yet also rejecting Paul as too Jewish, is also historical.

The translation of the German hymn excerpts are the playwright's, with the exception of "A Mighty Fortress is

Our God." Ideally, they should be sung to the melodies that would have been used in that time and place (specifically the Silesian melody for "Fairest Lord Jesus"), as they differ slightly from the melodies found in American hymnals. However, use of the American hymnal versions is acceptable.

Actors should use their native accents, as opposed to artificial German accents. The word "amen" may be pronounced "ahmen" or "aymen," as long as it is consistent among the actors.

THE CONFESSING CHURCH, *a play in Two Acts* by Rachel Lulich, was originally presented at Lake Bible Church, Lake Oswego, Oregon on June 1 & 2, 2018 with the following cast of characters:

KARL FASSLER: Marty Beaudet
JOHANN MITTLER: Brett Daniels
ANJA RICHTER: Lainie Alexander
JEW 1: Luke Nelson
JEW 2: Kara Thiringer
ARYAN JESUS: Kristofer Bromander
INGRID KELLER: Katie Mortemore
ERIK UHLMAN: Jerald Rose
HEINRICH EHRHARDT: Max Miller
GEORG RICHTER: John Dotson
HELENE RICHTER: Brenda McGinnis
MARTIN STEIN: Nathan Baloga
DR. HELMUT SCHAF: Barry Kennedy
REPORTER: Kara Thiringer
GUARD: Luke Nelson

Characters
in order of appearance

Karl Fassler: Anja's professor of world religions. Early 50s.
Johann Mittler: Anja's classmate. 20.
Anja Richter: A college student. 21 years old.
Jew 1: The conniving Jew stereotype.
Jew 2: The idiot Jew stereotype.
Aryan Jesus: A fabrication of the "German Christians."
Ingrid Keller: Anja's childhood friend. 21.
Erik Uhlman: Pastor of Lutheran Redeemer Church. Mid-30s.
Heinrich Ehrhardt: The head elder at Lutheran Redeemer Church. 60s.
Georg Richter: Anja's father, a WWI veteran. He relies on a cane. Mid-50s.
Helene Richter: Anja's mother. Early 50s.
Martin Stein: Anja's boyfriend, a seminary student. 24.
Dr. Helmut Schaf: Regional director of the German Christian Faith Movement. Attractive. Late 40s.
Reporter: A voice on the radio.
Thugs: A group of SA "brown shirts."
Guard: A prison guard.

Act I

SCENE 1

SETTING: Germany, 1930s.
AT RISE: A college classroom in tableau. FASSLER holds an open Bible, and JOHANN is seated. ANJA RICHTER stands apart, praying.

ANJA: Father, please be with me today. Give me courage. Help me respond to your leading. In Jesus' name, amen. (ANJA walks to the classroom and takes a seat, joining the tableau.)

SCENE 2

(JEW 1 and JEW 2 in exaggerated stereotype—hooked noses, etc—enter. They represent a manifestation to the audience of what is being taught in FASSLER's class.)

JEW 1: When he comes by—
JEW 2: He'll be here any minute!
JEW 1: —we'll have him!
JEW 2: How?
JEW 1: Taxes.
JEW 2: Taxes! Taxes?
JEW 1: I'll ask if we ought to pay taxes to Caesar.

Jew 2: A curse on his head!
Jew 1: If he says yes, he's a collaborator.
Jew 2: A curse on collaborators!
Jew 1: If he says no—
Jew 2: A great man!
Jew 1: You idiot! If he says no, he's an enemy of the state. Do you see?
Jew 2: But... We hate Rome.
Jew 1: And who do we hate more than Rome?
Jew 2: ...
Jew 1: Jesus, you fool! When he comes by, we'll ask him the question. Either way he answers, he's condemned.
Jew 2: Look!

> (ARYAN JESUS enters. His long hair is blond and he is clean-shaven. His skin is fair. He is tall and strong; the picture of Aryan perfection.)

Jew 2: Ask him! Ask him!
Jew 1: Master!
Jew 2: Ask him!
Jew 1: Is it lawful to pay taxes to Caesar?
Jew 2: Taxes!
Jew 1: Should we pay them, or not?
Aryan Jesus: Why are you testing me, Jew? Bring me a coin.
Jew 1: Give me a coin.
Jew 2: Taxes!
Jew 1: Give me a coin!
Jew 2: Oh.

> (JEW 2 produces a coin. There is a brief struggle before JEW 1 pulls it from his grasp and hands it to ARYAN JESUS.)

Aryan Jesus: Whose image is on the coin?
Jew 2: A curse on his head!
Jew 1: It is Caesar's, Master.
Aryan Jesus: Give to Caesar the things that are Caesar's, and to God the things that belong to God.

> (Jew 1 and Jew 2 recoil, then Jew 1, Jew 2 and Aryan Jesus exit.)

Scene 3

> (Focus returns to the college classroom. Fassler resumes teaching his class, referencing the scene just manifested.)

Fassler: Here we see Martin Luther's two kingdoms doctrine in full force, as we discussed in our unit on Christianity—what belongs to Caesar and what belongs to God. The government shall concern itself with the former; the church with the latter. I also want you all to note the desire to entrap Jesus in Jewish anti-government politics. We can see the conniving nature of the Jews all through history, even today—it is a racial characteristic.
Johann: Professor Fassler?
Fassler: Yes, Johann?
Johann: How do we see it today?
Fassler: The most obvious way is their business dealings. We've seen, over the last several years, how they have continued to prosper while the rest of the nation floundered financially. Do you think that happens by accident? The cleverness of the Jews allows them to take advantage of situations and people to their own benefit.
Johann: Is that why they've been removed from public office?

Fassler: No, that has more to do with their foreignness. We Germans are Aryan, and the Jews are a completely separate people.

(Anja half raises her hand.)

Fassler: Still, it's true, they are unwanted wherever they go, and why? Because of their sneaking, invasive ways, like vermin.

(Students murmur agreement; Anja lowers her hand.)

Fassler: Everywhere they go they bring trouble. They are the great disease of mankind. Did you have a question, Anja?
Anja: ... No, Professor Fassler.

Scene 4

(The street. Ingrid hands out flyers as Anja walks home.)

Ingrid: Anja? (Anja is oblivious.) Anja! Is that you?
Anja: Ingrid! You're back!
Ingrid: How have you been? Are you still at university? Are you and Martin engaged yet?
Anja: Martin's still in seminary. He's doing research for one of his professors right now, so I'm taking summer classes.
Ingrid: That must be hard.
Anja: He's coming home for a visit next weekend. What about you? How was Berlin?
Ingrid: Here, take a flyer. Berlin was wonderful. It's such an amazing time to be alive, don't you think?

ANJA: (Reading flier.) You're part of the German Christian movement?
INGRID: Aren't you?
ANJA: I've heard of it, but I don't really know much about it.
INGRID: They've been organizing in Berlin for more than a year. We're putting an end to the church struggle, once and for all.
ANJA: How do you plan to end the church struggle?
INGRID: By uniting the churches under our new Imperial Bishop. Our first local meeting is tomorrow night. Will you come?
ANJA: I don't know.
INGRID: Oh, please? I'm to introduce our speaker for the evening, and I'm so nervous.
ANJA: You're introducing the speaker? In front of everyone? You?
INGRID: I know. But this is so important, Anja. It'd be nice to see a familiar face in the audience.
ANJA: Well...
INGRID: Please?
ANJA: Alright.
INGRID: Thanks. You're a real friend. (INGRID hugs ANJA.)
ANJA: I'd better get home. It's good to see you, Ingrid.
INGRID: It's been too long. I'll see you tomorrow. (Saluting) Hail Hitler!
ANJA: Bye. (ANJA starts to leave.)
INGRID: Anja. The proper response to "Hail Hitler" is "Hail Hitler."
ANJA: (A pause. Part salute, part wave) Hail Hitler.

SCENE 5

(ERIK UHLMAN and HEINRICH EHRHARDT are

in Uhlman's office at Lutheran Redeemer Church. UHLMAN hands EHRHARDT several copies of the German Church Constitution.)

UHLMAN: I saw Otto this morning, but if you'll pass these along to the rest of the Elder Board, I'd appreciate it. I'd like to discuss it at our next meeting.
HEINRICH: Certainly. So this is the new Evangelical Church Constitution.
UHLMAN: It's not nearly as bad as we feared.
HEINRICH: Good. Our Imperial Bishop hasn't consolidated his influence yet.
UHLMAN: He's mentioned, of course—Articles 5 and 6 outline his role and power, but the wording is specific. And Article 1 is a strong, clear statement of our basis in and responsibility to the Gospel, and that alone.
HEINRICH: Good. (Reading.) This last sentence is quite robust. There can be no mistake that the Church derives its authority apart from the State.
UHLMAN: Precisely.
HEINRICH: What did Otto say when you gave him his copy?
UHLMAN: Nothing. He said he'd read it at home.
HEINRICH: You can't fault a man for wanting to carefully consider something before reacting.
UHLMAN: It's secretive.
HEINRICH: Or wise.
UHLMAN: Maybe. Here. (He hands HEINRICH a paper.)
UHLMAN: It's a circular letter that's been making the rounds.
HEINRICH: (Reading the letter.) Who else have you shown this to?
UHLMAN: No one. I wasn't sure who to trust.
HEINRICH: Hmm. (He continues reading.) I like Bishop Adler, but this is a risky step.

Uhlman: It's a perfectly reasonable statement. And there are already several well-respected signatories.
Heinrich: And you're considering adding your name.
Uhlman: I'm considering it.
Heinrich: You'd be officially aligning yourself with the Confessing Church.
Uhlman: I think it's probably past time I did. With the German Christian movement on the rise and the increased persecution of the Jews, I can't in good conscience remain silent. I just don't know if this is the right way.
Heinrich: The Reich will certainly consider it anti-government. There could be severe consequences for you.
Uhlman: You think I should pass?
Heinrich: I think you should bring it before the Elders. We can discuss it properly, and you can make a decision with our counsel and support.
Uhlman: I appreciate that, Heinrich. But you're the chairman of the Elder Board. If the vote comes out in favor of me signing the letter, you could come under scrutiny, yourself.
Heinrich: It's possible.
Uhlman: I just don't want to take unnecessary risks.
Heinrich: It is hard to know what to do. We'll need to pray for guidance.

Scene 6

> (The Richter living room. Georg Richter reads the newspaper. Helene Richter reads a women's magazine. Anja idles over her homework. Georg closes the paper.)

Georg: It's a glorious day to be German. It reminds me of when I was young, before the war.

Helene: A glorious day, indeed.
Georg: Things are finally looking up, Helene. Where would we be without the new social programs? Scrabbling for cash that wasn't worth anything. Always under England's thumb. Not anymore.
Helene: To victory.
Georg: To victory. And may God bless Adolf Hitler. He's doing wonders for this country.
Helene: He's a brilliant leader.
Georg: I'll confess I had concerns at first; those Brownshirts...
Helene: They're in the minority, Georg.
Georg: He seems to have them in hand. I'm going for a smoke. Will you join me on the porch, Lene? (Georg rises.)
Helene: I'll join you in a moment. Up wind.
Anja: Father? What do you know about the German Christian movement?
Helene: It's an effort to finally unite the German churches. Everyone's been talking about it. Oh, Georg, there's a local rally tomorrow. We should go.
Georg: A good cause. I don't think it's likely to succeed, though.
Helene: Why ever not?
Georg: I just don't think the church struggle will end any time soon. Why do you ask?
Anja: I ran into Ingrid Keller today.
Helene: Oh, is she back from Berlin?
Georg: I thought she was going to stay there.
Helene: She was only gone a few months.
Anja: Almost a year, Mother.
Helene: Was it that long?
Anja: She was handing out fliers for the meeting. She said they're trying to unite the churches under the Imperial Bishop.
Georg: Really?

HELENE: And so they should.
GEORG: Well, maybe I was wrong.
HELENE: We're to obey the authorities placed over us.
GEORG: Maybe there's hope for unity, after all. (Exit Georg.)
HELENE: You seem out of sorts this evening, Anja.
ANJA: Difficult day in class.
HELENE: I thought you might be missing Martin.
ANJA: I always miss Martin.
HELENE: When's he coming for a visit? I miss him.
ANJA: Mother.
HELENE: He's smart, handsome, and has a lovely voice. He'll make a fine preacher. And he'll make somebody a fine husband.
ANJA: I'm sure he will. I'm going for a walk.
HELENE: Don't stay out too late.
ANJA: I won't. (ANJA kisses HELENE on the cheek and exits.)

Scene 7

(MARTIN, with a letter to ANJA.)

MARTIN: Dearest Anja, I have exciting news! My hermeneutics professor, Dr. Kohl, has invited me to participate in a major research project. It's a collaborative effort—half the faculty is involved. Only three students have been brought on board so far, and I'm the youngest, so you can imagine how nervous I feel! But Dr. Kohl has assured me that he requested me himself. He and I are quite like-minded in our approach to biblical interpretation, so perhaps I shouldn't be so surprised by my selection. We'll be working intensely for the next few months, and I'm afraid I won't be able to visit as planned. It will all be worth it in the end, though. I can't tell you much about the project, but I want you to understand its significance. We will be giving the German people a revolutionary new edition of the Bible! I know you'll understand, and share my excitement. With love, Martin.

Scene 8

(Uhlman's office. UHLMAN is kneeling on the floor, praying. GEORG approaches, ready to knock. He sees UHLMAN and waits.)

UHLMAN: Amen. (He sees GEORG, and gets up.) Mr. Richter. How are you? How's the old war wound?
GEORG: Oh, same as ever. It doesn't trouble me much. (They shake hands and sit.)
UHLMAN: What can I do for you?
GEORG: I've heard some talk—and I know gossip is the devil's work, but I only heard it—I heard you went to a lecture by that fellow, what's his name? Young fellow, like you. Theologian. Spent some time abroad.
UHLMAN: You mean Mr. Bonhoeffer.
Georg: Bonhoeffer, that's it. Is that true?
UHLMAN: Yes. It's no secret.
GEORG: But you haven't made it known.
UHLMAN: I've never felt the need to report my every movement to the congregation.
GEORG: I'm not suggesting that you should. But in times like these—I know opinions can be very sharp.
UHLMAN: Is yours?
Georg: I have no opinion—I don't know anything about this fellow.
UHLMAN: Then why have you brought it up?
GEORG: I thought you ought to know people are talking.

Uhlman: I see.

Georg: Well, you know, nothing squelches gossip quicker than the subject finding out about it.

Uhlman: You're a good man, Mr. Richter. I'm glad to have you in my congregation.

Georg: I've sat under your teaching for eight years. I've never had reason to complain. Of course, if you deserve to be chastened, you deserve to be chastened, but make it public. I won't have people talking about you behind your back. And as far as I know, there's no harm in going to a lecture.

Scene 9

> (A German Christian rally. Ingrid, helmut Schaf, Helene, Georg, Uhlman, and Anja are all present.)

Ingrid: Ladies and gentlemen. Thank you for attending our first local German Christian rally. We are so glad to see you all. We come together tonight with a shared vision. A vision of cooperation and peace. Cooperation as we unite the German churches under a single banner, and peace with our new government. This is the new Germany, and we are all a part of it. (Applause) It is my great honor to introduce our regional director, Dr. Helmut Schaf. Dr. Schaf.

> (Applause as Schaf takes his place at the front of the room.)

Schaf: My fellow Germans. This is our time. Our time to be one people, unified by soil and blood, and now, religion.

We are the German Christians, and under the leadership of Ludwig Müller, our newly appointed Imperial Bishop, all regional church institutions will be brought together into a single Imperial Church. (Applause) My friends and countrymen. The church struggle has gone on long enough. Why should we bicker about politics and policy? Why do we argue about semantics in the new church constitution? Why do Martin Niemöller, Dietrich Bonhoeffer, and the foreigner, Karl Barth, choose strife over unity? "A house divided cannot stand."

HELENE: (To GEORG.) That's true.

SCHAF: But it need not be this way. Our gracious Führer has given us the opportunity to come together by appointing Mr. Müller over the Protestant churches of Germany. He has provided us the means of reconciliation. When Adolf Hitler fought in the war, he was momentarily struck blind. Without the use of his natural sight, he nevertheless had a vision for the German people. He would raise us up out of the pit of despair that we were plunged into by our unjust defeat. He would save Germany and bring us into a glorious future—a new Reich that will last a thousand years.

INGRID: Hail Hitler!

ALL BUT UHLMAN: (ANJA quiet and late.) Hail Hitler!

SCHAF: My friends, my fellow Germans. When Paul met Christ on the Damascus road, he too, was struck with temporary blindness. He too, received a vision. And what did the Apostles do? Did they deny Paul entrance when he sought to join their ranks?

HELENE: No!

SCHAF: No, indeed! But what will we do? Will we sit back while others enjoy the Führer's glorious vision? Will we be quarrelsome? Will we deny him entry into our hearts? Let

it never be said that the German Church stood by bickering while the rest of the nation marched onward into glory!
HELENE: Amen!
ANJA: Mother.
INGRID: Hail Hitler!
SCHAF: To victory!
ALL BUT UHLMAN AND ANJA: To victory!

SCENE 10

(ANJA, with a letter to MARTIN.)

ANJA: My dear Martin, I received your letter today. Of course I am disappointed you must delay your visit. I was hoping to talk a few things over with you. I went to a German Christian rally last night. Ingrid Keller introduced the speaker—do you remember her? She used to be so shy. Do you know anything about the German Christians? I felt uneasy the whole time I was there, and some of the things they said were very concerning. I wish you were here, and we could walk along the river and debate the finer points of doctrine like we used to. I am thrilled for you, though—what a wonderful opportunity! I'm glad your professors have recognized your hard work. You said it's a new edition of the Bible. Are you updating the Luther Bible, or is this to be a new translation? I know you have been working very hard on your Greek. I'm so proud of you. Yours, Anja.

SCENE 11

(The sanctuary at Lutheran Redeemer Church. UHLMAN, HELENE, GEORG, ANJA, HEINRICH, and INGRID are present. They sing the last verse of "Praise to the Lord, the Almighty," hymnals in hand. They know it well; there should be harmony. INGRID should stop singing when they come to "Abraham's children.")

ALL: Praise to the Lord, let me praise him with all that is in me. / Let all that breathes join with Abraham's children in singing. / He is thy light, / O my soul, don't fear the night. / Praise the Lord, for he is holy. (All sit except UHLMAN.)

UHLMAN: 2 Timothy 1:7. "For God hath not given us the spirit of fear, but of power, and of love, and of a sound mind." Beloved congregation, we live in tumultuous times, but we ought not to live in fear. There are those who would, through intimidation, discourage us from living out our beliefs. They may speak of triumph, but we must not let them triumph in this. I believe some of you have expressed concern that I recently attended a lecture by Dietrich Bonhoeffer. Let me assure you that Mr. Bonhoeffer is a theologian of the highest order. While I cannot say I agree with everything he espouses, he is most certainly a man of God, and he is proclaiming the truth of God to all who will listen—we should all be so bold as he. As we read in 1 Peter 3:15, we should "be ready always to give an answer to every man that asketh you a reason of the hope that is in you," and, as it continues in verse 16, we must do this "with gentleness and the fear of God." Loved ones, do not confuse the reverent fear of God with the fearful dread of our fellow man. I exhort you, dear ones, not to live as though under that spirit of fear, but rather according to the spirit of God within you—of power over fear, of love for your fellow man, and of the sound mind of reason in the midst of all this chaos.

Scene 12

(Classroom in tableau. Jew 1 and Jew 2 talk amongst themselves.)

Jew 1: Look at him.
Jew 2: Look!
Jew 1: Did you see him earlier? He invited that tax collector to be part of his inner circle.
Jew 2: Tax collector?
Jew 1: Yes. Matthew, the tax collector—the Roman collaborator!
Jew 2: A curse on his head!
Jew 1: And now he's eating with him!
Jew 2: A curse on tax collectors!
Jew 1: Why does he eat with tax collectors and other sinners?
Jew 2: Disgusting.
Jew 1: Let's talk with his disciples. I can't imagine they're pleased about this.
Jew 2: Not pleased!

(Jew 1 and Jew 2 exit.)

Scene 13

(Focus returns to the college classroom. Fassler resumes teaching his class, referencing the scene just manifested.)

Fassler: Notice the Jewish obsession with money. How can we account for it? (Johann raises his hand.) Yes, Johann?
Johann: It's in their blood, isn't it, Professor Fassler? Even

in the Old Testament, they stole from the Egyptians as they left.

ANJA: What?

FASSLER: Anja. What else, Johann?

JOHANN: Could it also be because of their wandering?

FASSLER: Very good, Mr. Mittler. Wandering peoples have always been prone to greed, theft, and other moral failings; look at the Gypsies. The Jews are no different, (ANJA raises her hand.) and what else should we expect from people with no homeland? What would you like to add, Anja?

ANJA: Johann is mistaken, Professor Fassler. The Bible says the Egyptians gave the Jews all those things as they left. They didn't steal them.

FASSLER: And where does it say that?

ANJA: In the book of Exodus, sir.

FASSLER: The Old Testament. The books of the Jews. And who wrote the book of Exodus?

ANJA: Moses, sir.

FASSLER: Moses. And to what race did Moses belong?

ANJA: He was Jewish, sir.

FASSLER: He was Jewish.

ANJA: But, sir—

FASSLER: And what did Moses do before leading the Jews out of Egypt? He was raised by Pharaoh's daughter, was he not? Saved by her from certain death when his own parents—his Jewish parents—abandoned him. But was he grateful? Did he have any loyalty to the people who took him in and raised him as a royal son? No. He betrayed his adoptive family—his adoptive nation. He killed a man! And then he ran away. He was a murderer and a fugitive, and this is the man the Jews hold up as a model to follow. No gratitude. No loyalty. This is the man the modern Jew still admires.

(Johann sniggers.)

ANJA: ...

FASSLER: (to the class) This is exactly the sort of confusion that occurs when sacred texts are read as truth instead of literature. Make no mistake, class. There is only one truth: National Socialism, and we have only one savior: Adolf Hitler. Class dismissed.

(ANJA remains glued to her seat as the others exit.)

SCENE 14

(Uhlman's office at Lutheran Redeemer Church. UHLMAN stands looking out the window as ANJA approaches and knocks.)

UHLMAN: Anja! Come in.
ANJA: Hello, Pastor Uhlman. I hope I haven't disturbed you.
UHLMAN: A welcome interruption. Please. (They both sit.) To what do I owe the pleasure?
ANJA: Moses wasn't abandoned by his parents.
UHLMAN: I'm sorry?
ANJA: The basket; the river. They saved his life.
UHLMAN: Yes.
ANJA: Then he killed a man.
UHLMAN: I understand it was a few years later, but yes. He did.
ANJA: And then he ran away. He was a murderer and a fugitive.
UHLMAN: He also had a speech impediment.
ANJA: But God chose him.
UHLMAN: The burning bush, yes. I'm familiar with the text.

ANJA: When he went back to lead Israel out of Egypt, he was a different man than he had been before.
UHLMAN: That's right.
ANJA: (leans back in the chair) Why couldn't I say any of that?
UHLMAN: What happened?
ANJA: I'm taking a world religions class and we're studying Judaism right now. Professor Fassler was saying how horrible Moses was and how terrible it is that the Jews look at him as a hero, and I couldn't think how to respond. There was just—He said so many things that were wrong. I didn't even know what to respond to.
UHLMAN: I see. (Aside.) This is a dilemma we'll all be facing more and more.
ANJA: What do you mean?
UHLMAN: I'm no prophet.
ANJA: But you have concerns.
UHLMAN: It may all come to nothing. In the meantime, I advise prayer. You read your Bible regularly?
ANJA: Yes. Mostly.
UHLMAN: That's the best thing you can do: be in the Word, and pray—for wisdom and courage to speak.
ANJA: I did speak. I just don't seem to be any good at it.
UHLMAN: Don't fall into the trap of not speaking because of fear.
ANJA: But what if speaking only makes things worse?
UHLMAN: There are those who advocate prudence. They say... They call it "resistance by silence." The basic concept is that, by not supporting what everyone is being expected to support, we're showing our disapproval, and I think that's true to a degree. But the question then becomes, is that enough?
ANJA: Is it?
UHLMAN: To be perfectly honest, I've been asking myself that same question for months. I believe it is true that

speaking out may be the wrong course of action in certain circumstances. But I'm beginning to think more and more that we use that as an excuse to remain silent when we shouldn't. You felt compelled to speak?
ANJA: I tried.
UHLMAN: The Lord knows it. And he knows you'll try again.

Scene 15

(The Richter's living room. ANJA sits reading a book. GEORG reads the paper. HELENE enters, pinning on her hat.)

HELENE: Are you sure you won't come, dearest?
GEORG: It's chilly tonight. My leg prefers to stay here and rest.
HELENE: Anja?
ANJA: I have homework, Mother.
HELENE: Anja, this is history in the making! Surely that's more important than homework.
ANJA: Surprisingly not.
HELENE: Didn't you like that first rally, Anja? You were very quiet afterward, and you haven't come to any since.
ANJA: It was fine. I've been busy with school.
HELENE: "Fine?" A glowing endorsement.
GEORG: Leave the girl alone, Lene. There will be plenty of other rallies.
HELENE: I'll bring you both a program.

(GEORG and HELENE kiss. Exit HELENE.)

ANJA: Your leg prefers to stay here and rest?
GEORG: Didn't you finish your homework before dinner?

(They share a moment.)

ANJA: This is her fourth rally.
GEORG: We all need our hobbies.
ANJA: In less than two weeks.
Georg: It's good for your mother to have a few social activities now and then. You should go out once in a while. I haven't seen any of your friends all year.
ANJA: But the rallies?
GEORG: As long as I don't have to go, I don't mind.
ANJA: They're so...
GEORG: We went to one meeting—the first meeting. It's a little too political for my taste, but I'm sure they've calmed down.
ANJA: I just don't think it's—
GEORG: Anja. Don't worry so much. Your mother has a level head on her shoulders. Let her enjoy herself.

SCENE 16

(German Christian rally. SCHAF speaks from the front of the room. HELENE and INGRID in attendance.)

SCHAF: Brothers and sisters of German blood, never before has the German Church faced so monumental a task. If we are to be a Church in the midst of the people, we must be a Church for the people—for our own people.
INGRID: For Germany!
SCHAF: Our new government wishes to cooperate with us fully, if we will only cooperate with them. Fellow Germans, we languished under the democracy of Weimar. But now we have been given new life in Hitler. The Church must rise up alongside the Führer to bring the people into uni-

ty—one land, one race, and one Church, that the nation will flock to once again.
HELENE: (saluting) Hail Hitler!
ALL: Hail Hitler!
SCHAF: How will we do this without unity among ourselves? We must align ourselves unconditionally with our Imperial Bishop. Adolf Hitler himself reached down and raised Ludwig Möler from obscurity—we must help him establish his authority. We must also align ourselves with National Socialism in a commitment to Positive Christianity—we will stand together in service to our nation, not insisting on archaic doctrines in a spirit of negativity. We must stand together in opposition to the Bolsheviks, the pacifists, and the Jewish materialists. We will cast off the corrupt 19th century ideas of racial equality, and recognize the differences between the races, as God created them. And we will educate our children, so that they will understand the debt they owe to their heritage as the Aryan people of Germany.

(Applause.)

HELENE: Amen!
SCHAF: My fellow Germans, will you join with me in pledging yourselves to the service of your local parish; to work on behalf of the poor, to give to the needy, to defend the faith, even if our own local pastors should be our attackers? Will you pledge yourselves to Positive Christianity? To be a truly German Church? Will you?
ALL: We will!

SCENE 17

(Uhlman's office. Enter UHLMAN and HEINRICH.)

Uhlman: Praise God.
Heinrich: Amen.
Uhlman: (Throws himself into a chair.) It wasn't unanimous.
Heinrich: But it passed. You can sign the circular letter on behalf of the church.
Uhlman: I'm glad I didn't have to cast a tie-breaking vote. I thought there might be more opposition in light of Romans 13.
Heinrich: You brought up good biblical examples of obeying God above earthly authorities.
Uhlman: Still. It's a relief. And Otto voted with us!
Heinrich: I told you he wasn't being secretive.
Uhlman: You were right. (He picks up the letter and considers it a moment.)
Heinrich: It's perfectly reasonable.
Uhlman: But not without risk.
Heinrich: As we discussed. But we've prayed for wisdom, and your elders are behind you.

> (A pause. Uhlman takes up a pen and signs the letter.)

Scene 18

> (Martin, with a letter to Anja.)

Martin: My dearest girl, I was so pleased to receive your letter. I miss you very much. I have not engaged with the German Christian movement myself, so I cannot comment on your discomfort, but I believe they have noble goals. Unity in the Church would be a welcome change from all this turmoil. As for our project, it is not an update of the Luther translation, but beyond that I cannot tell you. Know that I am doing well, and that we are making excellent headway. I have high hopes for its completion within the next few weeks. With love and fondness, Martin.

Scene 19

(Classroom in tableau. Jew 1, Jew 2, and Aryan Jesus enter.)

Jew 1: He has to be stopped.
Jew 2: Trouble-maker.
Jew 1: You can't just walk into the temple and throw a fit. He had no right to chase out the moneychangers.
Jew 2: No right!
Jew 1: We must put a stop to this.
Jew 2: Let's catch him!
Jew 1: But how?
Jew 2: ...
Jew 1: We'll have to challenge his authority. That's the only way. Who is he, anyway? A carpenter from Galilee.
Jew 2: A pox on Galilee!
Jew 1: Quiet. (He approaches Aryan Jesus.) Master. By whose authority do you teach?
Jew 2: Beelzebub!
Aryan Jesus: Tell me, Jew, under whose authority was John the Baptist working? God's, or man's?
Jew 1: ... A moment. (Jew 1 and Jew 2 withdraw in a huddle.) If we say John's authority came from God, Jesus will ask us why we didn't believe him.
Jew 2: A crazy man!
Jew 1: But we can't say his authority came from men, because the people consider John a prophet—it will make them angry.
Jew 2: Prophet! Was he?

Jew 1: They may even stone us.
Jew 2: Stone us!
Jew 1: Stop that!
Aryan Jesus: What is your answer, Jew? Did John baptize with the authority of heaven or of man?
Jew 1: Master, we cannot tell.
Aryan Jesus: Then I will not tell under whose authority I act.
Jew 2: A curse on his head!

(Jew 1, Jew 2 and Aryan Jesus exit.)

Scene 20

(Focus returns to the college classroom. Fassler resumes teaching his class, referencing the scene just manifested.)

Fassler: Note the dishonesty of the Hebrew. They do nothing sincerely, always striving for power over the people around them, ever intolerant of revolution. But as an Aryan, Jesus had a very different mindset from the Jews.
Anja: The Pharisees.
Fassler: Miss Richter?
Anja: Jesus had a different mind set from the Scribes and the Pharisees. And he was not Aryan.
Fassler: I think you'll find that he was.
Anja: Why are you doing this?
Fassler: I am merely relating the story.
Anja: You're twisting it.
Fassler: Miss Richter, I am explicating the text for the sake of students who have never read it with a critical eye.
Anja: It's a simple passage.
Fassler: And yet, clearly able to be misinterpreted.

ANJA: Clearly.
FASSLER: Be very careful, Miss Richter. Your performance in this class has been dismal as it is. I advise you to maintain a respectful tone. Do you understand?
ANJA: (A long pause.) I apologize for my tone, Professor Fassler. But I cannot allow you to misrepresent Christ.

(Silence.)

FASSLER: You are dismissed.

SCENE 21

(The sanctuary of Lutheran Redeemer Church, as before. The congregation sings the final verse of "Fairest Lord Jesus," hymnals in hand.)

ALL: All of the beauty / in earth and heaven / is composed in thee alone. / Nothing on earth should / become more precious / than thee, the one who saves my soul.

(All sit except UHLMAN.)

UHLMAN: Acts chapter 4, verses 18 and 19. "And they called them, and commanded them not to speak nor teach at all in the name of Jesus. But Peter and John answered and said unto them, Judge for yourselves, whether it be right in the sight of God to hearken unto you more than unto God." Beloved congregation, since the fall of man there has always existed a tension between heaven and earth. And while we believe that God is sovereign and ordains who is in power in every time and place, this does not mean they have a divine right to rule in any way they choose. Our leaders, like us, are accountable before God Almighty. This week, your Elder Board voted on the signing of a circular letter, which acknowledges the truth of our individual and corporate responsibility to obey God above all earthly powers. I will read it for you, so that you may all know where your church leadership stands with regards to this issue. If you have any concerns, please see me or Heinrich Ehrhardt.

"We, the undersigned, acknowledge the biblical importance of submitting to earthly authorities as outlined in Romans 13:1 and 1 Peter 2:13-15. However, we also acknowledge the fact that such obedience may be limited or overridden when the Church, her mission, or the free preaching of the Gospel of Christ are threatened. Such is the case in Acts 5:29, and in the example of Jesus, himself. As stated in Article 1 of the German Church Constitution, we are ultimately responsible to a higher authority than the State. The current Church struggle reminds us of the necessity to obey the State unless and until it causes the Church to violate the law of God."

Scene 22

(Anja, with a letter to Martin.)

Anja: Dearest Martin, I don't understand why you can't tell me more about your project, but I trust your judgment. I'm glad you have the chance to help bring it to completion. Regarding the German Christians, their intentions may be good, but I question the nobility of their goals. Still, Father thinks the first meeting was mostly bluster, and I know if you were here you would encourage me to look more deeply before coming to a conclusion. I will attend another rally. I wish you were here to go with me and talk it over. I miss you. Anja.

Scene 23

(German Christian rally. INGRID and SCHAF greet people at the door. Enter ANJA and HELENE.)

INGRID: Anja! I'm so glad you came back.
ANJA: Hello, Ingrid.
HELENE: Dr. Schaf? Dr. Schaf, this is my daughter, Anja.
SCHAF: It's a pleasure to finally make your acquaintance, Miss Richter. (They shake hands.) I'm pleased you could join us this evening. It's been difficult for your mother, always coming alone.
HELENE: I hope Georg will come again, now that Anja has.
INGRID: I'm sure he will. Come in and take a seat, we're just about to start.

(They take their seats. Ingrid sits next to ANJA. DR. SCHAF takes the stage.)

Ingrid: I'm so glad you're here, Anja.
SCHAF: My fellow Germans. Tonight's rally will be quite special. You all know how our mighty Führer has mobilized our young people for the cause of Germany. Tonight, we will hear from an outstanding young woman. She has worked with the German Christian movement for the past year, first in Berlin, and now here. You have seen her each week, and heard her open each rally. Now, she will give the evening's message. Ingrid Keller.

(Applause. INGRID rises and takes her place on stage, while DR. SCHAF sits.)

INGRID: My German brothers. My German sisters. We have achieved so much.
HELENE: (to ANJA) Isn't this exciting?
INGRID: We have begun our movement in earnest. And our Führer has heard our cries.
HELENE: Our little Ingrid.
INGRID: We have an Imperial Bishop. We have a new Church Constitution, though it fell short of our hopes.

(The crowd murmurs in agreement.)

HELENE: You should spend more time together.
ANJA: Mother.
INGRID: Brothers and sisters, we are joined by the blood of our people. We are the German Church, and the Church must reflect its membership. We will complete the work that Martin Luther started. We will have a revolution. A revolution to create a German Church, independent of all others. You have heard it said that the Church is universal, crossing all the natural boundaries of blood and soil, but I say to you, that the German Church is German: One nation, one race, one Church!

(Applause.)

INGRID: Ours is a racially distinct experience of the Divine, and we will not be sullied by the inclusion of other races.

(Applause.)

INGRID: How are we to win our countrymen over unless we turn away from all that isn't German in our worship? Are

we to greet them with a Jewish Old Testament in violation of the racial experience of faith?
ALL EXCEPT ANJA: No!
INGRID: We cannot! We will not hold to texts soaked in the blood of barbaric animal sacrifice. We will not accept the explanation of some that this ritual is an image that points us to Christ. We reject the notion that we need a scapegoat. We reject the Jewish idea that there is a natural separation between God and man. We reject the false doctrine of original sin, and proclaim the truth that the only way man and God are separated, is when man deliberately sets himself apart from God.
HELENE: Amen!
INGRID: The evils of theology are revealed in its attempt to force us to believe we need the salvation offered through the Church. Brothers and sisters, we are a pure race. We will not be deceived by the lies of men like Karl Barth, Dietrich Bonhoeffer, and our own bishops and pastors. They will tell you the foundation of Christianity is Judaism, but is it so?
ALL EXCEPT ANJA: No!
INGRID: They will tell you the Old Testament is part of the Christian Bible, but is it so?
ALL EXCEPT ANJA: No!
INGRID: Brothers and sisters of our ancient Germanic blood, they will tell you that all have sinned and fallen short of the glory of God, but is it so?
ALL EXCEPT ANJA: No!
INGRID: It is not so!
HELENE: To victory!
INGRID: To victory!
SCHAF: Hail Hitler!
ALL EXCEPT ANJA: Hail Hitler!

Scene 24

(The Richter's living room. Georg sits reading the newspaper. Enter Anja, followed by Helene.

Helene: Really, Anja. I wish you wouldn't walk so fast.
Georg: How was the rally?
Helene: Oh, Georg. You should have been there. It was inspired. Ingrid gave the message.
Georg: Ingrid? Anja's friend?
Helene: Yes, Ingrid Keller. If you would come to the rallies you would know who she is. Wasn't she was brilliant? It really was incredible, Georg. Do you remember how shy she was as a girl? You wouldn't recognize her. Would he?
Anja: I hardly recognize her, myself.
Helene: You see?
Georg: What did she talk about?
Helene: The movement, the Church of Germany. It was invigorating.
Anja: Mother, what did you think of her comments about Martin Luther?
Helene: Moving.
Anja: But they were inaccurate.
Helene: I don't know what you mean.
Anja: Luther wasn't creating a German Church for the Germanic race.
Helene: Nonsense. Luther was always very nationalistic. Why do you think he translated the Bible into German?
Anja: Because he thought everyone should be able to read the Bible in their native tongue, and German was his native tongue.
Helene: History was never your strong suit, Anja. You take too simplistic a view.

Georg: Is this really important?
Anja: What about the Old Testament?
Helene: Nobody reads the Old Testament, dear.
Anja: I do!
Helene: Do not take that tone with me, young lady. You haven't given the German Christians a chance. Right from the beginning you've been judgmental and unwilling to listen. When you agreed to come to the meeting tonight, I hoped you were beginning to see reason, but I see now that I was wrong. Don't set yourself against us, Anja. We have God and the Führer on our side, and we will prevail. (Exit Helene.)
Anja: Tell me again why I shouldn't worry about Mother.
Georg: Don't take that tone with me, either, young lady.
Anja: Did you hear any of that?
Georg: I heard several things without context.
Anja: Father, they reject original sin, they reject the need for salvation—they reject Romans 3:23!
Georg: Is it possible you're exaggerating a little?
Anja: I heard it with my own ears. If you had come to the rally like I asked, you would have heard it too—in context—and you'd know I'm right.
Georg: Listen, Anja, these German Christians are just trying to bring—
Anja: They're not Christians at all! Have you heard anything I've said tonight? They reject the very foundations of the faith! And mother—! (A pause. Exit Anja.)

Scene 25

(Uhlman's office. Uhlman sits at his desk. Heinrich holds a piece of paper in his hand.)

Heinrich: I wouldn't advise it.

Uhlman: I know.

Heinrich: Preaching from the Old Testament is not acceptable. They put Bishop von Tecklenburg under house arrest for it. And Franz Ewerlin was beaten in the street for using the pulpit to remind everyone that Jesus was a Jew.

Uhlman: I've heard of several such incidents. And worse.

Heinrich: Is that why you wrote this? Because nothing's happened to you?

Uhlman: No.

Heinrich: (Sets the paper on the desk.) You're a pastor. You have a congregation to think of.

Uhlman: I know. But I've been too cautious.

Heinrich: What will happen to the church if something happens to you?

Uhlman: I have to have faith that God will provide.

Heinrich: Any man can be a martyr, Erik. But we're not supposed to seek it out.

Uhlman: We're not supposed to avoid it, either. Not at the expense of truth.

Heinrich: (A pause.) You've made up your mind, then?

Uhlman: Will it put you at risk, Heinrich? As chairman of the Elder Board?

Heinrich: You're not in the habit of showing me your sermons ahead of Sunday morning.

Uhlman: But I did this time.

Heinrich: Only the outline. If they ask, I can honestly tell them I advised you not to preach it.

(They understand each other.)

Uhlman: I believe I have been called to do this.

Heinrich: Then you can do no other.

Scene 26

(Martin, with a letter to Anja.)

Martin: My dearest Anja, I cannot tell you how much your support and understanding have meant to me over the last few weeks. I know I haven't written as often as I should. You've been very gracious. Our work here is nearly done. I cannot wait to show you what we've created. This is the most significant update to the biblical canon since Martin Luther and Johannes Gutenberg. I believe this new edition of the Bible will have a dramatic impact, not only on the Church in Germany, but around the world. I'll try to bring a prototype with me when I come home—I'm sure Dr. Kohl will allow it. I long to see you again. I have missed you. With love, Martin.

Scene 27

(A radio announcement.)

Reporter: It is with great sadness and indignation that we must announce the death of Ernst vom Rath, a German embassy official in France. He was killed by a Polish Jew, demonstrating the eternal violence of his race.

Scene 28

(The street. The windows of Jewish storefronts are shattered. The sound of breaking glass, raised voices, and sirens in the background. Enter Anja.)

Anja: Oh, Lord. What is happening?

(Enter JOHANN. He wears a Swastika arm band and his hands are full of loot.)

JOHANN: Anja?
ANJA: Johann Mittler? What are you...?
JOHANN: Did you hear the news? That Jew murdered a German diplomat in France.
ANJA: I heard, yes.
JOHANN: We're teaching them a lesson.
ANJA: Johann. That was one man.
JOHANN: It's never just one man. Didn't you learn anything in class? World Jewry is a disease.
ANJA: They're people, Johann. And you're vandalizing their businesses.
JOHANN: They're a lower order of people. No wonder you failed the class. You don't understand anything.
ANJA: I understand that what you're doing is wrong.
JOHANN: It's sanctioned. I saw a Brownshirt in civilian clothes set fire to the synagogue.
ANJA: Sanctioned?
JOHANN: Yes. That is, the police aren't interfering, and nobody's been arrested except Jews. Don't you see? The German people have had enough, and now we're rising up against our Jewish oppressors, just like the Egyptians did.
ANJA: They're not oppressing anyone!
JOHANN: Don't try to argue, Anja. Your ignorance is embarrassing. (Exit JOHANN. A pause.)
ANJA: What should I do, Lord? What should I do?

SCENE 29

(ANJA, with a letter to MARTIN.)

ANJA: Dear Martin, as I write to you, the destruction continues for a second night.

(She pauses.)

Dearest Martin, I am so troubled by what is happening. I feel I am being torn apart. It's so wrong. Someone set fire to a synagogue last night. I heard there was a bucket brigade, so I went to see if I could help, but they weren't trying to save the synagogue; they were only preventing the fire from spreading to the surrounding buildings. I stayed out late. I just kept walking, listening to the sirens and the sound of breaking glass. I could hear it even from the river. My hair reeks of smoke. I should have done something.

(She pauses.)

Martin, I hope this letter finds you well. It is chaos here. Rioters set fire to the synagogue downtown last night, and I witnessed several shops being looted. Each time, I felt as though God were prodding me to intervene, but each time I walked away. What could I have done? I was scared, Martin. And now I'm sitting at home like a coward. (ANJA pauses once more, then crumples the paper in her hands.)

SCENE 30

(The sanctuary at Lutheran Redeemer Church, as before. The congregation sings the fourth verse of "O Sacred Head, Now Wounded," hymnals in hand.)

ALL: And what thou hast endured, Lord / is now my cross to bear; / I have myself to blame, Lord / and in thy death I share. / Behold, I stand before thee, / deserving of thy rage. / Grant me thine endless mercy, / and visions of thy grace.

(All sit except UHLMAN.)

UHLMAN: Esther 7:3-4. "Then Esther the queen answered and said, If I have found grace in thy sight, O king, and if it please the king, let my life be given me at my petition, and my people at my request: For we are sold, I and my people, to be destroyed, to be killed, and to be eliminated." Perhaps you remember the story of Esther; how Haman, the enemy of God, sought to destroy the Jews. And he nearly succeeded. But let us remind ourselves of the fate that he suffered, for King Ahasuerus listened to Esther and her uncle, Mordecai. Instead of a great slaughter of the Jewish people, Haman himself was hanged on the very gallows he had prepared for Mordecai, and all those who took up arms against Israel at Haman's prompting were killed by the very Jews they sought to murder, with the king's blessing.

(INGRID rises and exits.)

UHLMAN: Beloved congregation, do you not remember God's promise to Abraham in Genesis 12:3? "I will bless them that bless thee, and curse them that curse thee," and let us not forget how that verse ends: "and in thee shall every race on the earth be blessed." Dear ones, I did not know, when I chose this week's text, how very apt it would be. I did not know the violence our Jewish neighbors would suffer at the hands of the German race. I did not know that Herschel Rosenberg, a member of this very congregation, our brother in Christ, would be arrested and unable to join his family for our service this morning. Today, we mourn what little innocence our nation could hitherto claim before God.

Scene 31

(The Richter living room, empty. Enter Martin.)

Martin: Hello? Anja? Mr. and Mrs. Richter?
Anja: (Anja enters at speed.) You're home!

(They embrace and share a kiss. Enter Helene, followed by Georg.)

Georg: Martin!
Helene: Martin, you're back at last!
Georg: How are you, my boy?
Helene: Oh, let him breathe, Georg.
Martin: How are you Mrs. Richter? Mr. Richter? (He shakes Georg's hand.)
Georg: Sit down, take your coat off.

(Anja releases Martin, and he complies. They all sit.)

Martin: It's good to be back. I can't believe how long it's been.

(Martin kisses Anja.)

Anja: Did you bring the prototype?
Helene: Oh, Anja, let him settle in a moment.
Martin: No, she's right. I can barely sit still. (Martin removes a small, thin book from his coat pocket.) Look.
Georg: (Takes the book and starts leafing through it.) What's this?

HELENE: It's the project he's been working on, Georg. Don't you remember?
GEORG: Of course I do, I just thought it would be bigger.
ANJA: (Takes the book from Georg.) Is this the first installment?
MARTIN: It's complete. The new German Revised Bible.
ANJA: The whole thing?
MARTIN: This is just the prototype. The finished copy will be thinner.
GEORG: So it's just a portion of the book, then.
HELENE: He said it's complete, Georg.
GEORG: A complete edition of part of the Bible.
MARTIN: No, no. This is the new German Bible. In its entirety.
GEORG: But...
ANJA: You've left out the Old Testament.
MARTIN: And the works of Paul. Every trace of Jewishness has been excoriated. The Gospel narratives have been updated, as well, to reflect what we now know of Jesus' Aryan origin. I told you it would be revolutionary. It's the biggest project of its kind in history, and now it's finished. And I was a part of it! It's still hard to believe.
HELENE: It's extraordinary!
MARTIN: What do you think?

(Silence.)

HELENE: I had no idea you were involved in this, Martin. I heard about the project at the German Christian rallies, but Anja made it sound like you were just working on a new translation. I had no idea they were the same project. This is amazing! Anja, isn't this wonderful? Martin will be one of the preeminent Bible scholars in the nation because of this!

(A pause.)

MARTIN: She's speechless!
ANJA: You removed the works of Paul.
MARTIN: And the Old Testament, yes. We can finally say the Bible is a Christian text!

(A pause.)

GEORG: Congratulations on your achievement, Martin.
MARTIN: Thank you.

(A pause.)

GEORG: Helene, don't we have a bottle of wine in the pantry?
HELENE: Where are my manners? All this excitement! Look at Anja, still taking it in. If you'd come to the rallies, you wouldn't be so surprised. (Exit HELENE.)
GEORG: Martin, would you help her open the bottle? I want to take another look at this with Anja.
MARTIN: Certainly. (Exit MARTIN.)
GEORG: Anja? Are you alright?
ANJA: ...
GEORG: Anja?
ANJA: I can't believe it. How could he... This is...
GEORG: Misguided.
ANJA: No. It's a perversion.
GEORG: It's strange, true enough. But be calm, sweetheart, and think of everything that—
ANJA: Look what they've done.
GEORG: I know.
ANJA: They've defiled it. Claimed it as territory for the Reich.

Georg: Just consider what you're—

(Anja drops the book and exits.)

Georg: Anja?

(He watches her leave, then picks up the book. He doesn't open it. Enter Helene and Martin, each carrying two glasses of wine.)

Martin: Where's Anja?
Georg: She went for a walk.

(A pause.)

Martin: I'll go after her.
Georg: You'd better not.
Helene: She's been having headaches lately; and now all this excitement.
Martin: I should have prepared her.
Georg: Yes, you should have.
(Georg takes a glass from Helene and holds it up.)
Georg: Martin, you have truly succeeded in surprising us.
(He drinks.)

Scene 32

(Inter-cut scene. A street: Anja walks to the river and sits for a moment. She gets up and begins pacing. Lutheran Redeemer Church. Uhlman leaves his office. A group of SA Thugs enters and surrounds him. Anja gets on her knees and doubles over in tears and prayer.)

ANJA: Oh, Lord. Lord. Oh, Lord.

> (The THUGS attack UHLMAN, who tries to protect himself without fighting back. He is knocked to the ground and curls up in a self-protective ball while they beat him.)

ANJA: How can this be? God, how? Why?

> (The THUGS begin kicking UHLMAN.)

ANJA: Not Martin, Lord. Please. Not Martin. Take anything else from me. Not him.

> (The THUGS finish with UHLMAN. They take out cigarettes and light them for each other. UHLMAN doesn't move. Exit THUGS.)

ANJA: I'm sorry, God. Forgive me. I know you love me far better than anyone on this earth ever could. It's you or nothing. It always was. And in you, I have everything. Thank you. Thank you, Lord. I love you. I trust you. Please help me do this. Please help me. In the name of my Savior, amen.

SCENE 33

> (The Richter living room. MARTIN, GEORG, and HELENE are seated.)

MARTIN: Then once I've secured my first congregation, I'll ask Anja to marry me. Dr. Kohl has assured me that he'll give me a glowing recommendation, so I don't expect a long delay.

(Enter ANJA. MARTIN stands.)

MARTIN: Anja. You've been gone over an hour.
ANJA: I'd like to speak with Martin.
HELENE: We've been waiting for you to get back before talking about the Bible. I have so many—
ANJA: Alone.
HELENE: But Anja. We all want to hear about it.
GEORG: Helene.

(GEORG leads HELENE from the room. Alone, MARTIN moves toward ANJA, but she avoids him. A pause.)

MARTIN: What is it, Anja? Aren't you proud of me?
ANJA: This book you've created—
MARTIN: Well, helped create. I was one of many.
ANJA: Do you really call it a Bible?
MARTIN: This is the Bible, Anja, as it was always meant to be. Free from Jewish appropriation.
ANJA: Paul.
MARTIN: The Apostles never should have brought him into their midst.
ANJA: The Apostles were Jewish.
MARTIN: No, you see, that's what they'd have you think.
ANJA: "They?"
MARTIN: But it simply isn't so. The province of Galilee was Aryan! Then the Jews invaded and oppressed the people there, just like they did in Egypt. Jesus and his disciples were of those Aryan people.
ANJA: Do you even hear yourself? Nothing that you just said is historically accurate. Do you have any idea what you've done?

MARTIN: I don't think you understand what we've done. This is a gift—not just for Germany, but the world! As National Socialism spreads across the globe, so will Positive Christianity, and with it, the corrected Bible.
ANJA: National Socialism will never spread across the globe. God won't allow it.
MARTIN: That could be considered treason, Anja.
ANJA: Better treason than heresy.
MARTIN: You don't know what you're saying.
ANJA: This isn't Christianity, Martin. This isn't the Bible.
MARTIN: Anja.
ANJA: The Bible has 66 books in it, Martin. 39 in the Old Testament, and 27 in the New Testament.
MARTIN: You haven't been to seminary. You don't understand.
ANJA: I don't have to go to seminary to recognize heresy.
MARTIN: Don't preach to me.
ANJA: How could you do this? Did you ever believe at all?
MARTIN: How dare you question my salvation!
ANJA: What do you expect? You've mangled God's Word. You've twisted history and closed your eyes to the truth.

(MARTIN picks up his coat and puts it on.)

ANJA: I wish you could hear yourself—and the rest of the German Christians, too. You're believing in lies, Martin.
MARTIN: I feel sorry for you, Anja. You're too blinded by hate to see the truth.
ANJA: No, Martin. You're the one who's blind.
MARTIN: Give my regards to your parents. (He starts to leave.)
ANJA: Don't leave that book here.

(Martin retrieves the book and puts it in his coat pocket. He hesitates.)

ANJA: Goodbye, Martin.

(Exit Martin.)

FADE TO BLACK

ACT II

Scene 1

(Uhlman's office. U<small>HLMAN</small> sits at his desk, writing. His left arm is in a sling and his face still shows bruising. H<small>EINRICH</small> sits opposite, looking at a paper.)

H<small>EINRICH</small>: That's probably as much as we should do for now.
U<small>HLMAN</small>: I agree. It's not very—

(A knock at the door. U<small>HLMAN</small> and H<small>EINRICH</small> conceal their papers.)

U<small>HLMAN</small>: Come in.
A<small>NJA</small>: (Enters.) Good morning, Mr. Ehrhardt.
H<small>EINRICH</small>: Morning.
A<small>NJA</small>: Pastor Uhlman. It's good to have you back.
U<small>HLMAN</small>: Thank you.
A<small>NJA</small>: Do you have anything for me today?
H<small>EINRICH</small>: Yes. Erik?
U<small>HLMAN</small>: (Digs into a drawer and hands A<small>NJA</small> a single sheet of paper.) Thank you for doing this.
A<small>NJA</small>: Of course. (A<small>NJA</small> folds up the paper and slides it into her shoe.)
H<small>EINRICH</small>: How are you, Anja?
A<small>NJA</small>: I'm all right, thank you.
H<small>EINRICH</small>: And your parents?

Anja: They're fine.
Uhlman: Have you heard from Martin at all?
Anja: No. I don't expect to.
Heinrich: What of the German Christians?
Anja: The rallies are smaller and less frequent since they made their theology known at the national level. There are still plenty of adherents, though.
Heinrich: No one knows the heart of man but God. Your mother may yet come around.
Anja: In the meantime, she's an excellent source of information.
Uhlman: Anja.
Anja: I'd better get going.
Heinrich: Wait a moment. (Heinrich retrieves a basket with food and a Bible.) This is for the Rosenbergs. Would you be willing to deliver it to them?
Anja: (A pause.) Yes.
Uhlman: Are you sure? This is very different from distributing a sermon.
Anja: They could arrest me for the sermons just as easily as the basket. It's happened elsewhere.
Heinrich: You're more likely to be convicted for helping Jews.
Anja: Perhaps. But how can I say no?
Uhlman: (A pause.) They're staying with the Hoffmans. You know the address?
Anja: Yes.
Heinrich: (Gives her the basket.) There are some additional items sewn into the cloth. Make sure they know.
Anja: I will.
Uhlman: God be with you.
Heinrich: We'll be praying for you, Anja.
Anja: Thank you. (She doesn't leave.)

UHLMAN: Shall we pray now?

> (ANJA nods. UHLMAN moves to place his hand on her shoulder. HEINRICH rises and takes her free hand in his as they bow their heads.)

UHLMAN: Heavenly Father, we praise you for your faithfulness. Although we are facing many dangers and trials, we know we are not unique. You have always cared for your servants, and we know you will care for us, even unto death, if that is your will. We pray for safety, but more, we desire strength and courage to accomplish all that you have called us to do. Be with us as we labor in the Word, and in the struggles of our neighbors. In Jesus' name, amen.
ANJA: Amen.

Scene 2

> (The Richter's living room. HELENE and INGRID have coffee together.)

HELENE: What else? Does Dr. Schaf have any plans for reinvigorating the movement?
INGRID: The movement needs no reinvigoration, Mrs. Richter. The true believers are as dedicated as ever. Those who have left are not our concern.
HELENE: I think some people may approach things more cautiously, Ingrid. We must ease them into it.
INGRID: I didn't mean to suggest that your family...
HELENE: Of course not.
INGRID: How is Anja? I saw her a few days ago in the street, but she didn't stop to say hello.
HELENE: She's... She holds her own.

Ingrid: Such a shame about Martin.
Helene: I haven't given up hope entirely. He's to come home for Christmas, and I know Anja misses him.
Ingrid: I had hoped to find her here today.
Helene: She's started working for the church in her free time, running errands for the deacons' committee. Of course it doesn't pay at all. But I think she enjoys it.
Ingrid: The deacons' committee?
Helene: Yes. She delivers things to families in need.
Ingrid: Is that all she delivers?
Helene: I think she delivered some flowers recently—one of our families lost a loved one. Why do you ask?
Ingrid: I just hope she isn't engaging in any illegal activities—without her knowledge, of course.
Helene: Illegal activities?
Ingrid: Pastor Uhlman is no friend of the new Reich. I only hope he isn't using her.
Helene: I'm sure he would never do such a thing. Pastor Uhlman may be wrong about many things, but I believe he is a man of integrity.
Ingrid: I'm sure you're right.

Scene 3

(Anja sits alone at the river. Enter Georg.)

Georg: I thought you'd be here. (He sits beside her. A pause.) I'm proud of you.
Anja: Why?
Georg: The way you stood up to Martin. I know it's been a few weeks, but you were hurt and I didn't want to make it worse by talking about it too soon. (Pause.) You know your mother and I were very fond of Martin. He's been almost

like a son to us. When the two of you started seeing each other, it was like a gift.
ANJA: Father.
GEORG: But when he came home with that book, I knew. I know my little girl.

(They embrace.)

ANJA: Why did I not see it? All those years we knew each other, arguing about doctrine... I was so blind.
Georg: We all were. He was intelligent and honorable. He had every one of us fooled—including himself, I think. But it's not what a man says he believes that counts; it's what's in his heart.
ANJA: What about Mother?
GEORG: I don't know.

SCENE 4

(Uhlman's office. UHLMAN works with the door open, an open Bible and other books on his desk. FASSLER, in an SS officer's uniform and carrying a briefcase, comes to the door and knocks. JOHANN accompanies him, in an enlisted SS uniform. UHLMAN stands.)

UHLMAN: Good afternoon. Can I help you?
FASSLER: Are you Erik Uhlman?
UHLMAN: Yes, I am.
FASSLER: Good.

(FASSLER enters the office and seats himself. JOHANN takes a standing position in the room. While

Fassler talks, he places his briefcase on the desk on top of the Bible, pulling out a folder. Uhlman sits.)

Fassler: I am Lieutenant Fassler of the local SS unit. Perhaps you are aware that we've taken over from the SA?
Uhlman: I didn't know that.
Fassler: Since the Führer has disbanded the SA, it falls to us to maintain order throughout the Reich. I am here to review your report.
Uhlman: My report?
Fassler: When you arrived at the hospital, you said you'd been beaten by a group of men in SA uniforms. Is that correct?
Uhlman: It is.
Fassler: Excellent. You'll be happy to know that the situation has already been dealt with. Do you have any objections to the matter being dismissed?
Uhlman: I don't suppose there's any point in pursuing it.
Fassler: Good. (He replaces the folder in his briefcase, pulls out another, and opens it.) Now, regarding the sermon that provoked the attack, I understand you preached on the book of Esther following the Night of Broken Glass. Is that true?
Uhlman: (A pause.) I thought the matter was dismissed.
Fassler: The matter of the attack, yes.
Uhlman: I see.
Fassler: Did you preach from the Old Testament?
Uhlman: I did.
Fassler: For what reason?
Uhlman: It's a part of the Bible. I do periodically preach from it.
Fassler: You claim that you were not attempting to undermine the Reich with inflammatory preaching?
Uhlman: Sir, I understand your job is to ask questions.

Mine is to preach the Word of God to my congregation. In season and out of season.

FASSLER: Of course. But why not adhere to the Reich-approved program of Positive Christianity?

UHLMAN: Sometimes Christianity is positive. But sometimes it must look at the world and say "no."

FASSLER: I'm very troubled, Mr. Uhlman. My records show that you declined to swear the loyalty oath to the Führer. Your preaching has become increasingly aggressive toward the Reich and all it stands for. And then there's this. (He pulls out a sheet of paper.) There have been a number of circular letters making the rounds of Confessing Church pastors. This one seems to bear your signature. (He hands the letter to Uhlman, who looks at the signature block.) Is that your signature, Mr. Uhlman?

UHLMAN: It is. (He hands the letter back.)

FASSLER: Hmm. (FASSLER puts the paper back into the folder. He closes the folder and tosses it into the briefcase. He leans back in the chair.) Are you aware that in some districts, signers of letters such as that have been prosecuted? Some have been jailed.

UHLMAN: I am aware.

FASSLER: Then let us understand each other. Stability is paramount to the Furhrer at this time. But I like you. I'm going to give you a second chance.

UHLMAN: A second chance?

FASSLER: You are an intelligent man, Mr. Uhlman, and you've already seen what can happen if you're not careful.

UHLMAN: I have.

FASSLER: My men can offer you protection. Of course, I already have several sitting in on church services around the city. But if you'll agree to limit your sermons to safer topics, I can assign you a personal security detail.

Uhlman: (A long pause.) That's a very generous offer, Lieutenant.
Fassler: Anything to support the church.
Uhlman: I'm afraid I cannot accept.
Fassler: Well, I can't say I'm not disappointed. I was told you might be uncooperative, but I hoped our little chat might help you see reason. You won't reconsider?
Uhlman: No.
Fassler: Very well. (Fassler stands, and shuts his briefcase. He holds out his hand to Uhlman, who stands to shake it.) Thank you for your time, sir. I'll see myself out. Mittler.

(Exit Fassler. Johann steps forward.)

Johann: Mr. Uhlman, you are under arrest for signing an anti-government document.

Scene 5

(A radio announcement.)

Reporter: Today, the Jewish financial cartel has succeeded in bringing war to Europe, and indeed the world. Britain and France have declared war against Germany, and Australia and New Zealand have joined their alliance. Four nations have pitted themselves against one in a cowardly act of unprovoked aggression. Every citizen must stand ready to do his duty for his country: man, woman and child. But do not fear. Our mighty Führer will save us with an outstretched arm; he will give us victory over all our foes. Hail Hitler! To victory!

Scene 6

(The sanctuary at Lutheran Redeemer Church, as before, except that Ingrid is absent and Heinrich stands in Uhlman's place. The congregation sing "Holy God, We Praise Thy Name," hymnals in hand.)

All: Lord, have mercy, have mercy, O God; / Let thy blessings come upon us. / All thy promises for our good / Have revealed thy lovingkindness. / Lord, our hope is in thee alone; / Do not let us be lost and forlorn.

(All sit except Heinrich.)

Heinrich: 1 John 4:7 and 8. "Beloved, let us love one another: for love is of God; and every one that loveth is born of God, and knoweth God. He that loveth not knoweth not God; for God is love." I have here a letter from our pastor, which he has asked me to read to you today. "Beloved congregation, 'let us love one another,' for this is the exhortation of God. Our nation is at war. Our neighbors will experience fear, despair, anger; even hatred, and so will we. In such an atmosphere, it is imperative that we demonstrate our love for one another. Is it any wonder we are at war? Can we doubt the reason for it? Can we stand back in shock at God's decision to allow us to face the consequences of our actions? We cannot, for it is only too clear that we, as a nation, deserve this war. And since we cannot stop it, let us, as the Church of the Living God, stand in the midst of the darkness as a bright light of faith, hope, and love. Let us therefore remember each other often in prayer. Let us remember that we are to love our enemies. Let us remember that for us, 'there is neither Jew nor Greek, there is neither slave nor free, there is neither man nor woman; for you are all one in Christ Jesus.' Let us remember the Lord, and his lovingkindness."

Scene 7

> (The Richter living room. Georg reads the paper while Helene does needlework. Enter Anja.)

Anja: I'm going to the church. I'll be back before dinner.
Helene: Anja. Wait a moment, please. Put the paper down, Georg.

> (He peers over the top of the paper.)

Anja: What is it, Mother?
Helene: Anja, I don't think you should be making deliveries for the church anymore.
Anja: Why not?
Helene: Well, with Pastor Uhlman under arrest for treason, people might think you're involved.
Anja: Pastor Uhlman was arrested for signing an ecclesiastical document that was approved by the Elders.
Helene: I don't want you associated with his subversive activities.
Anja: I make deliveries for the deacon's committee, Mother.
Helene: Do you?
Georg: Helene?
Helene: Before Pastor Uhlman went to jail, did he ever ask you to do anything illegal as part of your work for the church?
Anja: Pastor Uhlman would never ask me to do anything wrong.

HELENE: That is not what I asked.
ANJA: It's what you should have asked.
GEORG: Anja, don't take that tone with your—
HELENE: It's all right, Georg. Anja? Did he ever ask you to do anything illegal?
GEORG: Why are you asking her? Anja would never do anything foolish.
HELENE: I had coffee with Ingrid Keller a few days ago. She expressed concern that Pastor Uhlman might be using Anja's work for the church to conduct illegal activities without her knowledge.
ANJA: What did you tell her?
HELENE: That Pastor Uhlman is a man of integrity and would never use my daughter in that way. But now that he's been arrested, I must admit I have my doubts.
ANJA: You told Ingrid the truth, Mother. Pastor Uhlman would never use me to conduct illegal activities without my knowledge.

(A pause. GEORG sets the paper down.)

HELENE: Did he ever ask you outright to do something illegal?

(Silence.)

GEORG: Anja. We have a right to know.
ANJA: So Mother can tell Ingrid?
GEORG: So we can protect you. Punishments are always worse in times of war.

(Silence.)

HELENE: It doesn't matter what you've done.
GEORG: It most certainly does matter.
HELENE: Georg. Whatever you have done up to this point, I am willing to forget it. But we are at war now! Pastor Uhlman could be executed if found guilty! I want you to promise me that from now on, you will obey the law in all things.
ANJA: Mother.
HELENE: You must promise me.

(Silence.)

GEORG: Anja?
ANJA: I will only promise to obey God.
GEORG: God commanded us to obey the authorities placed over us.
ANJA: A point clarified in the letter Pastor Uhlman signed.
HELENE: You're so fond of the Old Testament, Anja. What about the Ten Commandments? What about "honor thy father and thy mother?"
ANJA: In the New Testament, Jesus says if we don't love him more than even our own families, we cannot be his disciples.
HELENE: What if you're caught?
ANJA: Then I will face the consequences of serving God, and him alone. Just like Pastor Uhlman is doing.
HELENE: Is it so horrible to obey the law for the sake of safety?
ANJA: Daniel thought so.
GEORG: You're not being asked to renounce your faith, Anja.
ANJA: I'm being asked to worship a false god in Hitler.
HELENE: Anja, we're being serious!
ANJA: So am I!
GEORG: All right. All right!
HELENE: We're worried about you. We love you.
ANJA: I know what can happen, Mother. I know. But I truly

believe this is what God would have me do, and I am done giving in to fear.
Helene: Anja, listen to reason—
Anja: I am! I am listening to reason, which tells me it is wrong to persecute the Jews. Reason, which tells me I cannot ignore the law of God. No matter the consequences.

Scene 8

(Uhlman's prison cell. Uhlman talks to Heinrich through the bars.)

Uhlman: The state lawyer says none of the other pastors have been sentenced to death for signing the letter, so he doesn't think I will be, even being at war. I'm more likely to spend a few years in a concentration camp.
Heinrich: There's no chance they'll release you?
Uhlman: None.
Heinrich: Not even to put you under house arrest?
Uhlman: No. I'll certainly be convicted. It's alright. My ministry will continue wherever they send me.
Heinrich: Do you need anything?
Uhlman: (Holds up a Bible.) You've already brought it.
Heinrich: Do you have anything for me?
Uhlman: Here. (He hands Heinrich a letter.) For my parents. They've been in touch?
Heinrich: They have. They're praying for you. I'll bring you their letters as they arrive.
Uhlman: Thank you, Heinrich.
Heinrich: Of course. (He checks for Guard and leans in closer, lowering his voice.) Anything more?
Uhlman: I have something for Anja to distribute, if she's willing. Another sermon.

Heinrich: I'm sure she will be.
Uhlman: Just remind her that the language in these could be construed as treasonous.
Heinrich: I will.
Uhlman: I'm reminding you, too, Heinrich. You don't have to take it.
Heinrich: I can always tell them I thought it was just another letter. I haven't read it, after all.
Uhlman: I imagine it's only a matter of time before they come after you.
Heinrich: We did have a few guests in the congregation last week who did not seem happy with the sermon.
Uhlman: SS?
Heinrich: They've increased their surveillance of churches.
Guard: Time's up!
Uhlman: I'll pray they don't search you. Thank you for the Bible.
Heinrich: Lord, strengthen this man for what lies ahead. May you be glorified in his suffering.
Guard: Out!
Uhlman: God be with you.

Scene 9

(The street. Anja carries a basket of food. Enter Ingrid, opposite.)

Ingrid: Anja! How are you? I haven't seen you in so long. Why haven't you come to any more of our rallies?
Anja: Hello, Ingrid.
Ingrid: Your mother looked so forlorn at our last meeting, all alone again.

Anja: I've been busy. It's a new term, and I'm volunteering at church.
Ingrid: That's very good of you, Anja, but you ought to give the German Christians another try. We're cooperating with the government to provide for those in need.
Anja: I just don't think it's for me, Ingrid.
Ingrid: I know we were never very close. But I always liked you, Anja. You were nice to everyone. I would hate to see you get into trouble.
Anja: I don't know what you mean.
Ingrid: I think you do.
Anja: I need to be going.
Ingrid: Of course, you have deliveries to make.
Anja: Would you like to search the basket?

(Silence. Anja begins to leave.)

Ingrid: Anja. It looks suspicious, delivering things for a church where the pastor's been arrested for treason. You should be careful.
Anja: I appreciate your concern. But it's unnecessary.

Scene 10

(Fassler, with Johann.)

Fassler: We have a serious propaganda problem. Someone has been duplicating and distributing treasonous sermons. I believe we're looking for a student at the university, probably a member at a local church. (He hands Johann a file.) Inside is our list of suspects. I believe you know a few of them?
Johann: (He flips the file open and glances at the names.) Yes, sir.

Fassler: Find out who it is, and arrest them.

Scene 11

(Uhlman's prison cell. UHLMAN is asleep. From off stage ANJA, HEINRICH, and other congregants sing "A Mighty Fortress is Our God," waking UHLMAN. All actors remain off stage, except UHLMAN.)

All But Uhlman: A mighty Fortress is our God—
Uhlman: (waking) What?
All But Uhlman: A bulwark never failing—
Uhlman: (Laughs)
All But Uhlman: Our helper he, amid the flood—
Uhlman: Thank you, Lord.
All But Uhlman: Of mortal ills prevailing—
Uhlman: Thank you, Lord.
All But Uhlman: For still our ancient foe—
Guard: Enough of this! Leave immediately!
Heinrich: You are holding our pastor here. We're merely trying to boost his spirits.
Uhlman: God bless you.
Guard: This is a facility for political prisoners. You are not permitted to be here. Go home.
Heinrich: (singing) And though this world, with—
All But Uhlman: Devils filled / Should threaten to undo us—
Guard: Leave!
All: We will not fear, for God hath willed—
Guard: Silence!
All: His truth to triumph through us: / The prince of darkness grim / We tremble not for him—
Guard: Men!

ALL: His rage we can endure—
GUARD: Remove them!
ALL: For lo, his doom is sure—

(A commotion; the singing becomes uneven.)

ALL BUT UHLMAN: One little word shall fell him.

(More commotion; the party is broken up. Silence.)

UHLMAN: (singing) Let goods and kindred go, / This mortal life also; / The body they may kill: / God's truth abideth still, / His kingdom is forever.

SCENE 12

(The street. ANJA carries a few text books. Enter JOHANN and GUARD.)

JOHANN: Anja!
ANJA: Johann. I hardly recognized you in uniform. Have you left university?
JOHANN: Restrain her. (GUARD grasps her arms and JOHANN takes the books. He holds them by the edges of the spine, one by one. Leaflets fall out. He picks one up and reads.) Anja Richter, you're under arrest for treason.

(GUARD handcuffs her.)

ANJA: It's just a sermon, Johann.
JOHANN: It's anti-government filth! I knew it was you. Lieutenant Fassler thought so, too.
ANJA: Fassler?

JOHANN: Bring her.

(Exit all.)

SCENE 13

(Intercut Scene. INGRID, at the German Christians' meeting place. Enter HELENE.)

HELENE: Ingrid! Where is Dr. Schaf?
INGRID: I'm afraid he's out of town. What's the matter?
HELENE: It's Anja. She's been arrested!
INGRID: Arrested? I told her...

(Fassler's office. Enter FASSLER and GEORG.)

GEORG: Thank you for seeing me.
FASSLER: Always a pleasure to assist our veterans. (He sits.) What's the trouble?
GEORG: My daughter.
INGRID: What's the charge?
HELENE: Treason!
GEORG: She's been arrested on a completely unreasonable charge of treason.
FASSLER: That's very serious. What is her name? Perhaps I can influence the court.
GEORG: Anja Richter.
HELENE: I must speak with Dr. Schaf.
FASSLER: Anja Richter. Yes. I am familiar with the case.
INGRID: Dr. Schaf has gone to the mountains for a much-needed rest. I have no way of contacting him.
FASSLER: I'm not sure what power you think I have, Mr. Richter.

Helene: Ingrid! You can help. You're Anja's friend!
Fassler: The charges in your daughter's case are very serious.
Ingrid: I don't know what I can do.
Georg: But, you said—
Fassler: I misspoke.
Helene: Surely you have access to somebody—someone with the Imperial Bishop's ear. He can put a stop to this!
Fassler: We must let the law run its course.
Ingrid: Mrs. Richter, you give me too much credit. I am only known locally.
Georg: Sir, she's only a child. She didn't know what she was doing.
Fassler: The evidence suggests otherwise.
Helene: Please, Ingrid.
Georg: There must be something you can do.
Ingrid: There's nothing I can do, Mrs. Richter.
Fassler: I'm afraid your daughter is beyond my help. You'll have to rely on the defense attorney assigned by the State.

Scene 14

(Anja's prison cell. Anja lies on a cot. Guard and Helene enter.)

Guard: Richter.

(Anja rises and sees Helene.)

Guard: You have five minutes.

(Exit Guard. Helene and Anja meet each other at the bars.)

Helene: Your father and I tried everything.
Anja: I know.
Helene: We went to see city officials, the SS—everyone! I tried to talk to Dr. Schaf, but he's out of town.
Anja: I know, Mother. It's alright.
Helene: It's not alright.
Anja: You and Father did everything you could. It's alright.
Helene: ...
Anja: God could've changed my fate if he wanted. He still might.
Helene: What if he doesn't?
Anja: (A pause.) Then I'll die.
Helene: Are you not afraid?
Anja: I don't know. I was. But only of dying. I'm not afraid of death itself.
Helene: Could you not have cooperated, Anja? There's still time. You could tell them who you're working for.
Anja: No, Mother. I cannot do that.
Helene: But Anja—
Anja: I've already had to resist their questioning. Don't make me endure it at your hands, too.
Helene: (Conceding the point) I only want to save you.
Anja: I've already been saved, Mother. (A long pause.) I'm glad you came. I feel better.
Helene: You're my only child.
Guard: (Enters.) Time's up.
Anja: It hasn't been five minutes, has it?
Guard: Out.
Helene: Anja...
Anja: I love you.

(Exit Helene and Guard.)

ANJA: Please comfort my parents, Lord. Thank you for comforting me. Thank you. I ask that you would release me from this. But if not, give me courage to go willingly, just as your Son did. Let it bring you glory. Thank you for this peace. Amen.

SCENE 15

(The sanctuary of Lutheran Redeemer Church, as before, minus UHLMAN, ANJA, and INGRID. All are seated except HEINRICH.)

HEINRICH: John chapter 14, verse 27. "Let not your heart be troubled, neither let it be afraid." These are the words of Jesus to his Apostles, yet all of them were persecuted for following him, most unto death. In our own country, the lines have been drawn; the message made clear: We must align ourselves with the new regime, or face the consequences: Persecution. Imprisonment. Death. But there is nothing new under the sun, and like the early Christians, we may be "pressed on every side, but we are not distressed. We are afraid, but we do not lose heart. We suffer persecution, but we are not abandoned. We are oppressed, but we do not perish." Let us pray. Our gracious Lord. We pray for your sustaining grace and strength. We pray for your peace, that passeth all understanding. We ask for mercy for our enemies. Open their eyes, so that they might see what they are doing, and repent. Lord, help us suffer all things for you, who suffered all things for us. "For God so loved the world, that he gave his only begotten Son, that all who believe in him should not be lost, but have eternal life." We thank you for this, our great hope. In the name of Christ Jesus, amen.

Scene 16

(The Richter's living room. Georg and Helene.)

Helene: I have betrayed my child.
Georg: You didn't betray her.
Helene: I betrayed her trust.
Georg: So did I.
Helene: Is there nothing we can do?
Georg: We can pray, Lene.
Helene: I cannot.
Georg: Why not?
Helene: I have sinned against God.
Georg: He is faithful to forgive.
Helene: I cannot! (She exits.)

Scene 17

(Anja's prison cell. Anja kneels in prayer. Enter Guard.)

Anja: "For to me to live is Christ, and to die is gain." Thank you for your beautiful truth. I stand on the promises—
Guard: Richter. (Silence. The Guard bangs against the bars.) Richter!
Anja: Lord, lend me your strength and give me peace, for you are God. In Jesus' name, amen. Is it time?
Guard: They're waiting.

(Anja rises as he unlocks the cell door. She holds out her wrists to be handcuffed. She is calm. They both exit.)

Scene 18

(Intercut scene. UHLMAN, sitting in his cell, silently reads his Bible. GEORG, in his living room, is on his knees. HELENE enters part way through but lingers in the background.)

GEORG: "Our Father which art in heaven, Hallowed be thy name."

(A courtyard. Enter GUARD and ANJA, handcuffed. She walks without hesitating.)

GEORG: "Thy kingdom come. Thy will be done in earth, as it is in heaven. Give us this day our daily bread."

(Exit GUARD and ANJA.)

GEORG: "And forgive us our debts, as we forgive our debtors."
GUARD: (O.S.) Ready!
GEORG: "And lead us not into temptation, but deliver us from evil:"
GUARD: (O.S.) Aim!
GEORG: "For thine is the kingdom, and the power, and the glory, for ever."
GUARD: (O.S.) Fire!

(A volley.)

GEORG: "Amen."

CURTAIN

www.ingramcontent.com/pod-product-compliance
Lightning Source LLC
LaVergne TN
LVHW012127070526
838202LV00056B/5896